DATE DUE

GAYLORD			PRINTED IN U.S.A.

North, South, East, and West

By Allan Fowler

Consultants:
Robert L. Hillerich, Ph.D., Bowling Green
State University, Bowling Green, Ohio

Mary Nalbandian, Director of Science,
Chicago Public Schools, Chicago, Illinois

Fay Robinson, Child Development Specialist

CHILDRENS PRESS®
CHICAGO

Design by Beth Herman Design Associates

Library of Congress Cataloging-in-Publication Data

Fowler, Allan
    North, south, east, and west / by Allan Fowler.
      p. cm. –(Rookie read-about science)
    Summary: Gives a simple explanation of the four main directions
and tells how to use the sun to determine direction.
    ISBN 0-516-06011-2
    1. Cardinal points–Juvenile literature. [1. Cardinal points.
2. Orientation] I. Title. II. Series: Fowler, Allan.
    Rookie read-about science.
G108.5.C3F69 1993
526.6–dc20   92-39261
                                                CIP
                                                AC

When Carol walks to
school in the morning –
which way does she go?

She walks north.

The school is north
of Carol's house.

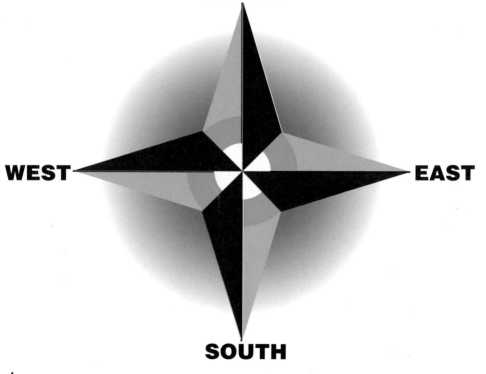

NORTH

When she goes home, Carol walks south.

NORTH

SOUTH

Since the school is north
of Carol's house,

Carol's house must be
south of the school.

At the same time that
Carol leaves for school,
her father leaves for work.

He rides a bus going east.

NORTH

EAST

SOUTH

NORTH

WEST

EAST

SOUTH

To get back home in the evening, he rides a bus going west.

North, south, east, and
west are directions –
the four main directions.

There are also in-between
directions.

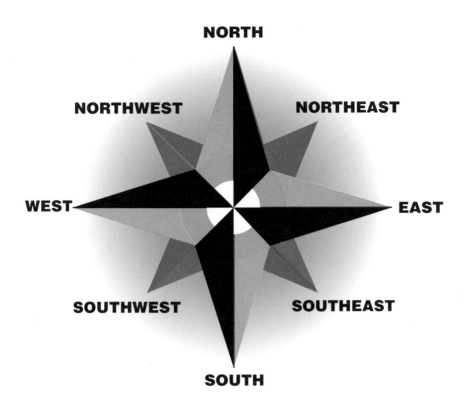

Like northwest, which is between north and west – and northeast, and southeast, and southwest.

It's easy to find directions.

Just remember, the sun always rises in the east –

and always sets in the west.

If you face the sun early in the morning, you're facing east.

If you face the sun as it
goes down in the evening,
you're facing west.

15

If you stand with your right hand pointed to where the sun rises, and your left hand pointed to where the sun sets —

you're facing north.

And if you turn around
so your left hand points
to where the sun rises,
and your right hand points
to where it sets –

you're facing south.

↑my school

↑my house

You can find a place if you know its direction, and how far it is from where you are.

Carol is visiting her aunt and uncle.

They told her they live three blocks east and two blocks south of Carol's house.

Now Carol can lead
the way!

Do you know what
direction your school
is from your house?

In what direction is
your best friend's house?

The supermarket?

The fire station?

It's a good thing that the sun always rises in the east and always sets in the west.

Because if it didn't, people would keep getting lost.

29

Directions

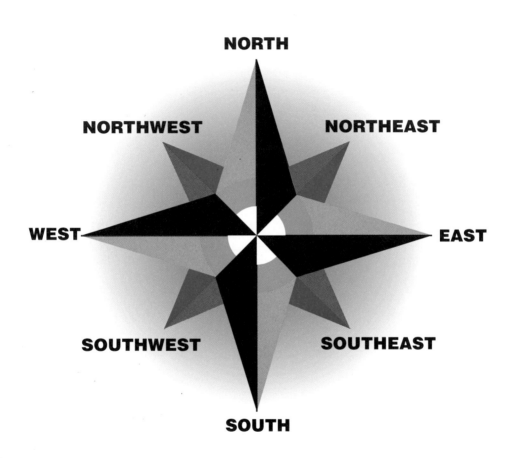

↑my school

↑my friend's house

↑my house

fire station

my aunt's house
↓

north
west ← → east
south

bus stop

supermarket

31

Index

About the Author

Allan Fowler is a free-lance writer with a background in advertising. Born in New York, he lives in Chicago now and enjoys traveling.

Photo Credits

PhotoEdit – ©David Young-Wolff, 3,5, 6, 8, 9, 17, 19, 23, 25, 26 (top right); ©Sven Wachli, 13; ©Michael Newman, 14, 15; ©Robert Brenner, 26 (bottom left)

Photri – Cover

SuperStock International, Inc. – ©L. Chiger, 12; ©S. Maimone, 26 (bottom right); ©G. Alter, 29

Illustration by Beth Herman Design Associates – 4, 11, 20, 22, 26 (top left), 30, 31

COVER: Weather Vane